TOOLS FOR CAREGIVERS

- **F&P LEVEL:** A
- **WORD COUNT:** 43

- **CURRICULUM CONNECTIONS:** counting

Skills to Teach

- **HIGH-FREQUENCY WORDS:** I, see
- **CONTENT WORDS:** ball(s), eight, five, four, nine, one, seven, six, ten, three, two
- **PUNCTUATION:** periods
- **WORD STUDY:** short a, spelled a (ball); long e, spelled ee (see, three); oo sound, spelled wo (two); r-controlled vowels (four)
- **TEXT TYPE:** information report

Before Reading Activities

- Read the title and give a simple statement of the main idea.
- Have students "walk" though the book and talk about what they see in the pictures.
- Introduce new vocabulary by having students predict the first letter and locate the word in the text.
- Discuss any unfamiliar concepts that are in the text.

After Reading Activities

First, begin by identifying items readers can see around them, such as pencils, books, or sneakers. Make a list of 10 items on the board. Then ask the readers to count how many of each object they can find around the room. Write their answers on the board. What is there the most of in the room? Of all the objects listed in the book, what is there the least amount of?

Tadpole Books are published by Jump!, 5357 Penn Avenue South, Minneapolis, MN 55419, www.jumplibrary.com

Copyright ©2020 Jump. International copyright reserved in all countries. No part of this book may be reproduced in any form without written permission from the publisher.

Editor: Jenna Trnka **Designer:** Anna Peterson

Photo Credits: Yarygin/Shutterstock, cover; Carlos E. Santa Maria/Shutterstock, 1; ilona75/iStock, 2; BrianAJackson/iStock, 3; Ronald Sumners/Shutterstock, 4; Adam Gilchrist/Shutterstock, 5 (tennis balls); Africa Studio/Shutterstock, 5 (raquet); LightFieldStudios/iStock, 6–7; wholden/iStock, 8; Liudmila Pereginskaya/Shutterstock, 9; Denise Lett/Shutterstock, 10–11; Olhastock/Shutterstock, 12; NickyBlade/iStock, 13 (candy machine); Birgit Reitz-Hofmann/Shutterstock, 13 (gum balls); Viren Desai/Shutterstock, 14–15; Anthony Rosenberg/iStock, 16.

Library of Congress Cataloging-in-Publication Data
Names: Peterson, Anna C., 1982– author.
Title: Let's learn counting / Anna C. Peterson.
Description: Tadpole books. | Minneapolis: Jump!, Inc., (2020) | Series: Fun first concepts
"Tadpole Books are published by Jump!" | Audience: Ages 3–6.
Identifiers: LCCN 2019031310 (print) | LCCN 2019031311 (ebook) | ISBN 9781645273141 (hardcover)
ISBN 9781645273158 (paperback) | ISBN 9781645273165 (ebook)
Subjects: LCSH: Counting—Juvenile literature. | Arithmetic—Juvenile literature.
Classification: LCC QA113 .P4664 2020 (print) | LCC QA113 (ebook) | DDC 513.2/11—dc23
LC record available at https://lccn.loc.gov/2019031310
LC ebook record available at https://lccn.loc.gov/2019031311

FUN FIRST CONCEPTS

LET'S LEARN COUNTING

by Anna C. Peterson

TABLE OF CONTENTS

tadpole
books

LET'S LEARN COUNTING!

I see one ball.

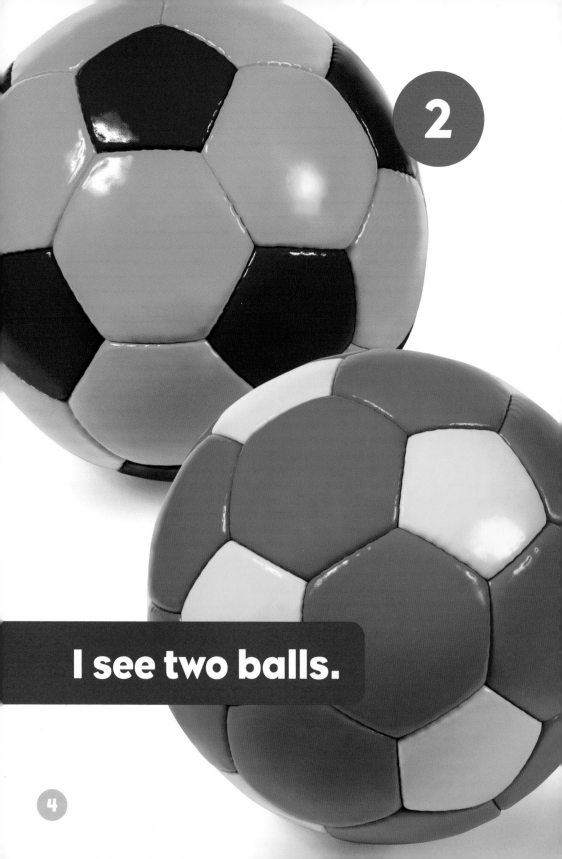

2

I see two balls.

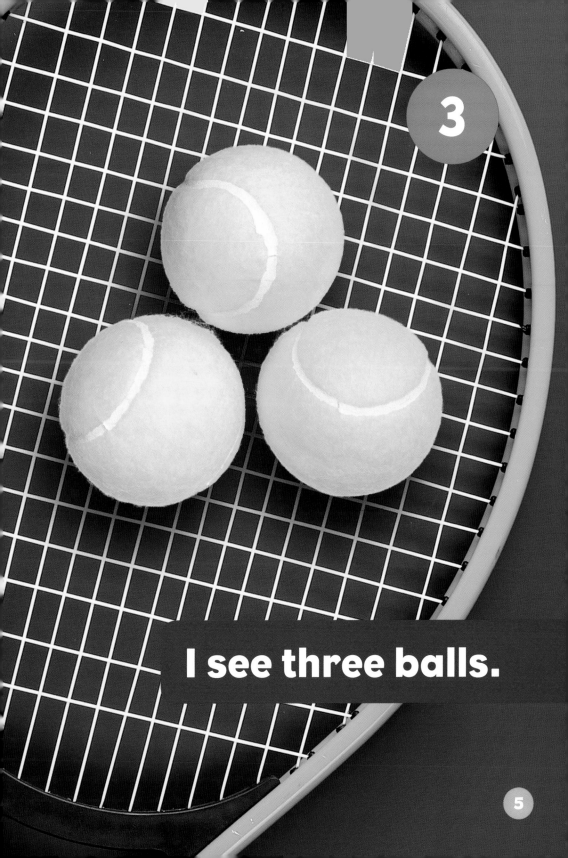

3

I see three balls.

I see four balls.

I see five balls.

6

I see six balls.

I see seven balls.

8

I see eight balls.

9

I see nine balls.

I see ten balls.

LET'S REVIEW!

How many balls do you see below?

NUMBER CHART

1 2 3 4 5

6 7 8 9 10